MW01504760

Cell Phones: Bringing the World Together

By
Chandler Tyrrell

Illustrated by
Lyle Miller

Columbus, OH

The **McGraw·Hill** Companies

Photo Credits

SRAonline.com

 SRA

Send all inquiries to:
SRA/McGraw-Hill
8787 Orion Place
Columbus, OH 43240-4027

Printed in the United States of America.

ISBN 0-07-604473-4

 2 3 4 5 6 7 8 9 MAL 10 09 08 07 06

Contents

Chapter 1
The World Is Calling

Imagine you're living before there was electricity—no TV, no radio, and no telephone. How did people communicate with one another before there were phones? Mostly they wrote letters to one another. Sometimes letters would take months to arrive, making communication extremely hard and slow.

Today telephones have become very important parts of our lives. We take for granted that we can immediately talk to someone by picking up a phone. Now that cell phones have been invented, our culture has changed quite a bit. It's possible to talk almost anywhere at almost any time.

In pre-cell-phone days, people could talk only on a phone that had a landline—a cord plugged into the wall. Inside the wall, a wire—or phone line—connects the landline phone to the rest of the system. Most people still have a landline phone, but they also have a cell phone.

Cell phones are a wireless improvement and can be used just about anywhere. People no longer have to stay in one place to make calls.

Landline phones were first used a little more than one hundred years ago in the late 1800s. At first only a handful of people had phones, and they could be used only in large cities because the lines connecting phones hadn't yet been prepared everywhere. However, as phones became more popular, new lines were constructed in more places, and about a hundred years later, phones were accessible to a billion people.

Cell phones have been catching on even more quickly. Only ten years after the invention of cell phones, a billion *more* people had these phones. Cell phones have become popular because they're so convenient and manageable. Because cell phones don't have cords, they work where landline phones can't. Now people can talk on the phone almost anywhere. Calls can be made and received from the side of a highway, from the middle of a lake, or from the top of a mountain.

In the United States about half the people own a cell phone. Many are even getting rid of their landline phones and choosing to use only cell phones.

In some European and Asian countries almost everyone has a cell phone. In these countries it's common for people to have no landlines—only cell phones. The reasons for this have to do with geography.

Landline phones are attached to wires, which are strung over land. In many places, running wires across the country is difficult and expensive. But cell-phone signals are sent through the air, and towers are used to send and receive the signals. These towers are simpler and cheaper to build than the structures needed for wires.

With the towers in place, communicating is much easier. There is wide agreement that the freedom to make a call anywhere is very desirable. This helps a country's economy grow, and people live better lives. For this reason and many others, cell phones are replacing many landline phones.

Perhaps you have a cordless phone at home. What's the difference between a cordless phone and a cell phone? Neither of them has a cord, so aren't they the same thing? Not quite. Cell phones are a little different from cordless phones.

Think about this: A cordless phone will usually work only at home—it's usually not possible for it to also work as close as next door.

This is because the cordless phone has to be close to a piece of equipment called a receiver, which plugs into the wall. The receiver connects the phone to the rest of the system. The cell phone, however, can be used wherever there's a signal— at home, next door, or in a different state.

Perhaps you're wondering how a cell phone works. It's very complicated.

Chapter 2
Why Is It Called a *Cell* Phone?

We'll start at the beginning. A cell phone is a two-way radio. One signal goes to a tower, and another signal goes from the tower to the phone. These independent signals let people talk and listen at the same time.

The tower is like the receiver for the cordless phone but much bigger. It takes calls from all cell phones in the area.

The area each tower covers is called a cell. Cell areas overlap so there are no gaps. This is where the name *cell phone* comes from!

A tower can take only a certain number of calls at a time (about fifty calls is the average), which is why cities need to have many towers. A big city needs an unbelievable number of towers to make sure cell phones aren't ineffective.

Cell areas can be bigger outside the city because fewer cell phones are used there. One tower in the country can cover many miles. Towers in the country environment are easy to see.

In the city, however, you may have the inability to see tower antennas because they're often on top of things that were already there, such as streetlights, flagpoles, and rooftops.

A cell phone is basically a radio that makes phone calls. Radios and landline phones, which send voices across long distances, are part of the cell phone's history.

Uncomplicated, sometimes incorrect forms of the telephone have been around for an unbelievably long time. One thousand years ago there was an incredible Chinese device historians think was a speaking tube.

Speaking tubes were used for hundreds of years. Have you ever talked into the end of a paper-towel roll? How does it make your voice sound? Speaking tubes work the same way. They run between the rooms and floors of a building or establishment. People who are far from each other can talk to each other indirectly and unseen through the tubes.

Another uncomplicated and inexpensive phone system used string stretched between two cups. When someone talks into one cup, it makes the string vibrate. The vibrations move through the string, and when the vibrations reach the other cup, the cup's shape amplifies the sound for the listener. The way the string carries moveable sound vibrations is similar to how an electric phone wire works.

A phone uses electricity to move signals along a wire. But the wire doesn't vibrate. Instead, the sound of a person's voice is used to change the way electricity flows in the wire. At the other end of the line, the changes are unscrambled back into sound.

Who invented the telephone? For years, innumerable historians thought it was Alexander Graham Bell.

Today historians know the inventor was an Italian named Antonio Meucci. In 1860 Meucci showed how a voice could be transmitted with electricity. But he didn't speak English; his discovery was written about only in Italian. Few people learned about it.

At this same time, other people were trying to show that it was possible to use electricity to send voices. But their devices were unsuccessful and ineffective.

Alexander Bell also was doing research and experiments. In 1875 he made a phone. A year later Bell made the first long-distance phone call to his friend, who was ten miles away! Bell brought his incredible device to the world's fair in Philadelphia. He didn't make the first phone, but he was the first to unveil it to the world.

Improvements were soon made to Bell's inconceivable telephone. Voices on the phone became clearer and louder, and wires were run all over the United States. In 1927 a call was made from New York City to London—over an entire ocean!

People were undeniably excited about telephones. But when did inventors first start to think about creating a cell phone?

Chapter 3
Part Phone, Part Radio

Today's phone system still uses wires to carry most calls. Landline phones send their signals through wires that connect to the phone system. But cell phones are radios, so instead they use something imperceptible called radio waves. Radio waves are invisible and move through the air, sort of like waves moving through water.

A radio transmitter is a piece of equipment that makes radio waves. But how do waves let you hear someone talking miles away? When a transmitter makes radio waves, the transmitter takes sounds—like the sound of your voice—and hides them in the waves. Then, when the waves are sent through the air, the sound of your voice is carried also. As improbable as it seems, your voice "flies" through the air!

As transmitters make waves, a radio receiver catches the waves the transmitter has sent through the air. Think of it this way: Imagine that you and your friend are standing in a big room. You write an important message to your friend on a piece of paper, and then you crinkle that paper into a ball. You throw that ball of paper across the room.

Your impatient friend catches the paper, uncrinkles it, and smooths it out. Your friend can now read the message you wrote. This is a little like how transmitters and receivers work, throwing invisible voice messages through the air on radio waves. This is also how cell phones work with radio waves—cell phones have both transmitters and receivers.

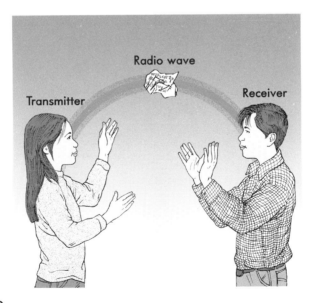

In the 1880s David Hughes created an instrument made of a battery and wires. He could turn electricity on and off in the wires, which meant he could make radio waves. Hughes saw that he could send sound signals with the radio waves.

He showed the device to other scientists, but they thought it was imperfect and didn't understand how it worked.

The other scientists thought Hughes wasn't really sending radio waves. They thought his device needed improvement, so they ignored his gadget.

In the next decade more devices like Hughes's were made, so it's unclear who actually invented the first radio. Some people think it was Nikola Tesla. He built a device in 1893 that worked just like radios people used years later. Tesla's device made a very great impact.

A few years later a man named Guglielmo Marconi built a radio that was like Tesla's. Marconi soon had an impressive factory making them, and for a long time many people thought Marconi invented the radio. But this story is like the story of Bell and the phone, because Marconi didn't invent the radio—he just independently unveiled it to the world.

Chapter 4
The Cell Phone Is Born

Ships were some of the first places where radios were used. People at sea could use the radio to communicate with those onshore, and this made ship travel safer. If something went wrong on a ship, it was possible for sailors to radio for help. Radios were good for talking to people on land, too, and for sending help over long distances. The world was becoming more connected.

In the 1920s police in Detroit put radios in their cars. These radios had an inability to send signals; they only received signals, which meant the police officers had to use phones to find out why someone had sent them a radio signal.

Soon police in other cities used these radios as well, and taxi drivers also found them helpful.

These first radios had a big problem. Signals crashed into each other. In 1927 a special group of people started making sure signals didn't crash.

Think of a highway. If there weren't lines on the road, people wouldn't understand where to drive and would crash into each other. In 1927 the special radio-wave group made sure radio waves traveled only where they were supposed to—through invisible road lines in the sky!

Another problem with the first imperfect radios was that they needed huge batteries.

However, during World War II in the early 1940s, the military created the walkie-talkie. The walkie-talkie uses small batteries and can be held in one hand. This technology was soon used in all radios.

Radios had many uses and helped many people communicate with one another. In 1946 the first dependable radios that could connect to the phone system were made.

But the special radio-wave group gave only a very small area in the sky to the radio waves for these radio phones. That area was much too small—only about twenty calls could be made at one time.

The idea for cell phones came from this problem. People had to figure out how to use that small, inadequate space in the sky to make many more than just twenty calls.

If you're really thirsty, do you drink just one tiny cup of water? No! You fill that cup over and over again. This is kind of how the scientists solved their problem. They figured out that to make more calls, they couldn't use each wave just once—they had to use the same waves over and over again. So, they made sure each tower in each area—or cell—reused waves.

Many responsible inventors worked on the idea of the cell phone. Then, in 1973, Martin Cooper made the first one.

In the 1980s cell phones were being used all over the world. People saw how impressive and convenient it was to always have a phone with them.

At the same time, phones were being made smaller. Then came digital code, which uses numbers to store lots of info in very small spaces. DVDs use digital code to fit movies onto small disks.

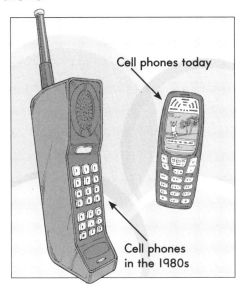

Cell phones today

Cell phones in the 1980s

Radio waves carry a lot more info when they're in digital code. Cell phones that use digital code in their radio waves can send much more info.

The code allows cell-phone users not only to make phone calls but also to send text messages and photographs. The Internet and e-mail also are available.

Cell phones are becoming more like computers. Most cell phones have video games and can save phone numbers and addresses. Some phones even keep notes. Soon many cell phones will be able to show Web sites on their screens. It probably won't be long before you can watch TV shows and movies on cell phones too. Unbelievable!

Cell phones were once used only by businesses, but now it seems almost everyone has a cell phone. The smaller cell phones become, the easier they are to carry. If you go on a walk, you'll probably see several people with cell phones. Now try to imagine all these people carrying big landline phones. That would be silly, uncomfortable, and inconvenient.

People in the future might remember today's pocket-size cell phones and think *they're* too big! There are already phones that don't need to be held! How? Many cars today have hands-free phones. Drivers use their voices to command the phone to dial someone's number, and the incredible phone dials on its own.

Chapter 5
Cell-Phone Awareness

In 2002 researchers showed that a phone could be put in someone's tooth! My goodness!

When the person on the other line talks, the phone's tiny speaker sends the sound through the listener's face bones and into the ear. But this phone only receives calls—the user is unable to send calls.

What will phones be like in the future? How will this affect how we communicate?

Today the world buzzes with the sounds of people talking to one another on cell phones, sharing ideas, experiences, and happiness in places they could never use a phone before.

But cell phones are still a new part of our world. People are still finding out what cell phones are capable of. They're finding both problems and answers with cell phones.

For example, some places have decided that cell phones are too disruptive and cause unfairness to other people. These places sometimes use a new technology called a jammer, which blocks cell-phone radio waves. This means it's impossible for cell phones to work in these places. Some movie theaters and schools now use jammers so that movies and classes will not be interrupted.

Another problem is old cell phones. In just one year, more than fifty million cell phones were no longer needed by their owners. Almost 25 percent of those phones were put in landfills.

However, cell phones have lead and mercury inside them, which are poisonous. Recycling cell phones may be the answer to cleanliness—making sure these terrible poisons don't pollute the ground.

There are other answers too. Many phone companies take old phones and reuse the parts. Some charities take old, incompetent phones out of kindness. First they update the phones, and then they give them to people who are unable to afford to buy them. This way, many people are fortunate to have a phone with them at all times in case there's an emergency.

In spite of these problems, cell phones have truly changed the world. Many years have passed since the first telephone was invented. Can you imagine the craziness people then might have imagined when they heard about something that could let them talk with someone who was miles away? Today we talk on phones—with cords and without—every day.

If inventors could combine a landline phone with a radio and create a cell phone, what likeness might inventors come up with in the future to improve the way people communicate? Will cell phones get better and better, or will scientists think of something completely different that allows people around the world to easily communicate?

Maybe someone you know has a cell phone. The next time you see the person using it, remember your cell-phone awareness. Think about the considerable time and work that went into making that phone. Think how a voice is changed into radio waves and sent to someone's ears. Cell phones have become an important part of our culture. The whole world is just a phone call away.